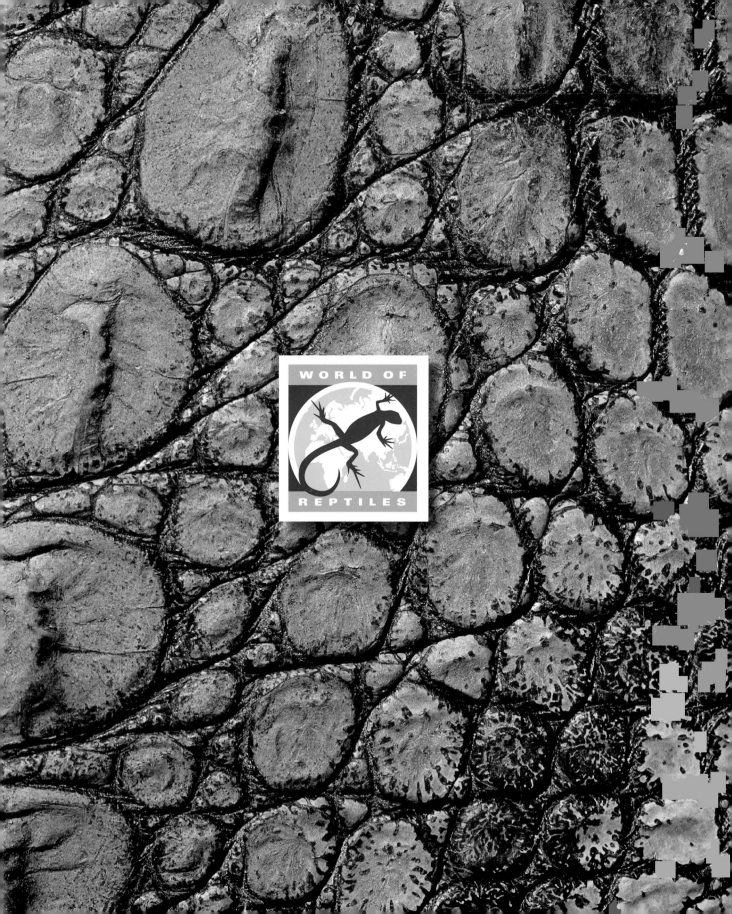

CROCODILES

by Sophie Lockwood

Content Adviser: Harold K. Voris, PhD, Curator and Head,
Amphibians and Reptiles, Department of Zoology,
The Field Museum, Chicago, Illinois

THE CHILD'S WORLD®, CHANHASSEN, MINNESOTA

CROCODILES

Published in the United States of America by The Child's World®
PO Box 326 • Chanhassen, MN 55317-0326 • 800-599-READ • www.childsworld.com

Acknowledgements:

The Child's World®: Mary Berendes, Publishing Director

Editorial Directions, Inc.: E. Russell Primm, Editorial Director; Pam Rosenberg, Editor; Judith Shiffer, Assistant Editor; Caroline Wood and Rory Mabin, Editorial Assistants; Susan Hindman, Copy Editor; Emily Dolbear and Sarah E. De Capua, Proofreaders; Elizabeth Nellums, Olivia Nellums, and Daisy Porter, Fact Checkers; Tim Griffin/IndexServ, Indexer; Cian Loughlin O'Day, Photo Researcher, Linda S. Koutris, Photo Editor

The Design Lab: Kathleen Petelinsek, Art Director, Cartographer; Julia Goozen, Page Production Artist

Photos:

Cover/2-3: Art Wolfe / Stone / Getty Images; frontispiece / 4: Pete Oxford / ImageState / Alamy Images.

Interior: Alamy Images: 23 (Bert de Ruiter), 27 (Gary Cook); Corbis: 5-top left and 8 (Frans Lanting), 5-middle and 16 (Michael Freeman), 12 (Tom Brakefield), 15 (Jonathan Blair), 19 (Jonathan Blair), 21 (Radu Sigheti / Reuters), 29 (Jonathan Blair), 30 (Charles and Josette Lenars), 34 (Nik Wheeler); Getty Images: 5-top right and 11 (Photodisc), 5-bottom right and 24 (David P. Redfearn / Photodisc), 5-bottom left and 37 (Photodisc).

Library of Congress Cataloging-in-Publication Data

Lockwood, Sophie.
  Crocodiles / by Sophie Lockwood.
    p. cm. — (The world of reptiles)
  Includes index.
  ISBN 1-59296-545-8 (library bound : alk. paper)
  1. Crocodiles—Juvenile literature. I. Title.
  QL666.C925L63 2006
  597.98—dc22   2005024787

TABLE OF CONTENTS

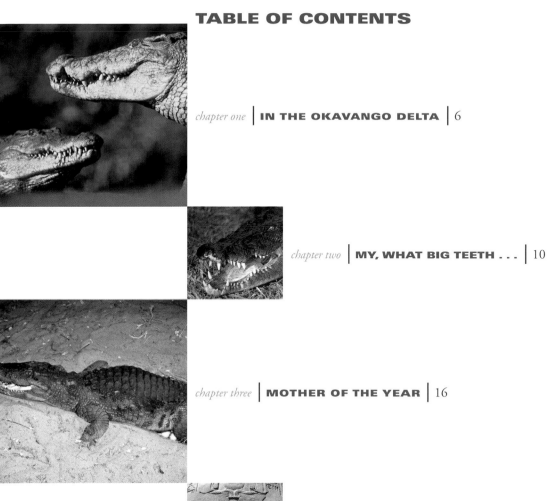

Chapter One

In the Okavango Delta

On the edge of the Kalahari Desert, in the far north of Botswana, lies the Okavango Delta. It is a swamp, a wetland paradise that borders one of the world's driest deserts. Okavango is crocodile heaven.

Crocodiles and lions are at the top of the Okavango Delta food chain. The lions prowl the dry land. The crocodiles dominate the riverbanks, lagoons, and waterways.

Hundreds of brilliantly colored bee eaters nest on the Okavango River's sand islands. Heron and egrets dip their long bills into the murky water searching for fish. Shy sitatungas slip through the papyrus reeds that grow in the Okavango wetlands, bending their heads to drink. In the shallows, hippos bob and snort. They leave the water at sunset to feed on nearby grasses.

Dozens of sleeping Nile crocodiles sun themselves on the riverbanks.

Nile Crocodile Fast Facts
(Crocodylus niloticus)
Adult length: 16 to 20 feet (5 to 6 meters)
Coloration: Dark olive to brown with darker, nearly black bands on the tail; lighter belly
Range: Africa below the Sahara Desert and along the Nile River
Reproduction: 40 to 60 eggs per nest
Diet: Fish, toads, frogs, snakes, turtles, antelope, buffalo, young hippos, wildebeest, and other mammals
International status: Threatened in Zimbabwe, Botswana, Kenya, Madagascar, Malawi, Mozambique, Tanzania, South Africa, Ethiopia, Uganda, and Zambia; endangered elsewhere

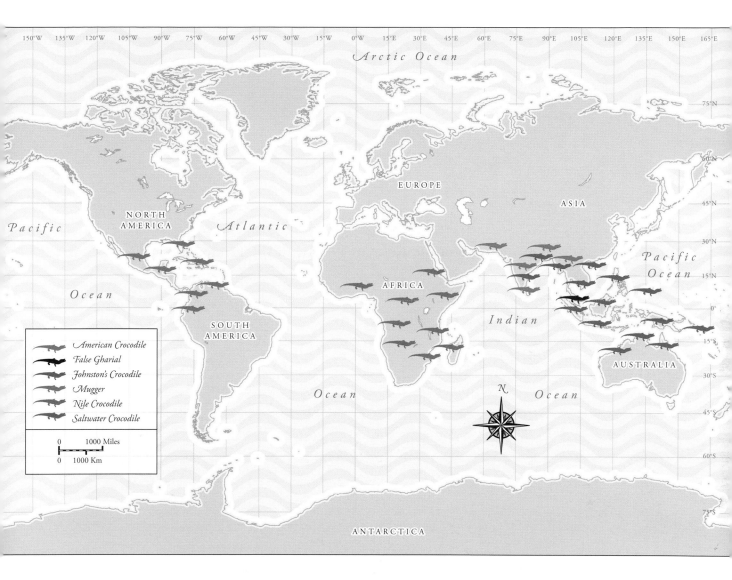

A huge granddaddy opens his mouth to yawn. He measures 20 feet (6 m) long, and weighs nearly a ton. Nile crocodiles are among the largest crocodiles in the world.

Crocodiles live throughout South and Southeast Asia, Northern Australia, the Caribbean Islands, South and Central America, and Florida.

Nearby, red lechwes drink at the river's edge. These antelope move easily through Okavango's marsh grasses. Their greatest enemies are lions. But today they need to

The Okavango River delta is the largest inland delta in the world. It is home to many animals including these two Nile crocodiles.

worry about crocodiles. The pond's water level is down, and the water is muddy. The lechwes must move farther into the water to drink.

A younger male crocodile lies still in the water as the lechwes approach. One careless beast comes too close, and the crocodile strikes. His powerful jaws clamp down on the lechwe's leg. It struggles desperately but cannot break the crocodile's hold. The croc spins its body around under the water, using its tail to guide the spin in what is called the death roll. Few creatures survive a crocodile death roll.

The crocodile's catch is large. The lechwe weighs nearly 250 pounds (114 kilograms). The croc drags his prey onto the riverbank, and the granddaddy slithers across the muck to share the meal.

Crocodiles do not need to eat as often as humans. About fifty meals a year is more than enough. The crocs of Okavango rarely go hungry. The waters teem with fish. Birds flock to the shorelines and nest among the reeds. Antelope, wildebeest, and more than 150 other kinds of mammals feed on the grasses and drink at the water holes. Nile crocodiles just wait for another meal to present itself.

Did You Know?
The Bayei people, an Okavango tribe, teach their children to fear the crocodile-filled waters where they live. The children learn this saying: "I am the river. My surface gives you life. Below is death."

Chapter Two

My, What Big Teeth...

Crocodiles are reptiles in the order Crocodylia. There are twenty-two or twenty-three species of crocodilians (scientists do not agree on the exact number). Species include crocodiles, alligators, caimans, and gharials. Crocodiles have long, narrow snouts. Their upper and lower teeth are visible when their jaws close. Alligators have broader snouts, and when their jaws close, only the upper teeth can be seen. Caimans look much like miniature alligators, their closest relatives. Gharials have extremely narrow, long snouts.

The fourteen crocodile species can be grouped by their length. Large crocodiles include saltwater, Nile, and American crocodiles. They measure about 16 to 20 feet (5 to 6 m). Medium-sized crocodiles, such as muggers and false gharials, range from 10 to 13 feet (3 to 4 m) long. Dwarf crocodiles, the smallest crocodiles, range 5 to 6.5 feet (1.5 to 2 m) long.

Each crocodile species has its own colors and patterns, size, diet, and chosen habitat. Some live in freshwater, while others are at home in salt water. All have long,

lizardlike bodies, four short legs with partly webbed toes, and a strong, muscular tail. Crocodiles also have unusual teeth, protective skin, a humanlike heart, and a digestive system capable of dissolving bones, hooves, and horns.

A crocodile's greatest weapon and most unique asset are its teeth. All crocodile teeth are cone-shaped but vary in size, depending on where they are in the mouth. Dwarf crocs have seventy-eight to eighty-two teeth despite their small size. Most medium and large crocodiles have sixty-four to sixty-eight teeth, with the exception of the false gharials, which have seventy-six to eighty-four teeth.

A crocodile has a thick, fleshy tongue attached to the floor of its mouth.

Teeth are lost and replaced throughout a crocodile's life. There is always a surface tooth in use. Beneath it lies a **successional** tooth. That tooth emerges when the surface tooth falls out.

False gharials have long snouts that are designed for catching fish, but they also eat other kinds of prey.

A thick, protective skin covers the crocodilelike armor on a medieval knight. Most crocodiles have bony plates embedded in some parts of their skin, called osteoderms. This word simply means "bony skin." Osteoderms protect crocodiles. Some crocodiles, such as the American crocodile, have few osteoderms. This characteristic has proved dangerous for American crocodiles because their smoother skins can be highly polished and used to make belts, shoes, wallets, and handbags.

Crocodiles digest their food in a two-chambered stomach. They have no molars for grinding food. Instead, the crocodile's first muscular stomach grinds its food. The second stomach contains powerful acid that digests the food for use in the crocodile's body. The crocodile's digestive system is able to remove all the **nutrients** from food.

The crocodile heart is much like a human heart. It has four chambers for pushing blood through the body. Unlike a human, however, a crocodile can control the amount of oxygen in its blood by closing a special valve and by increasing or decreas-

False Gharial Fast Facts
(Tomistoma schlegelii)
Adult length: 10 to 16 feet
  (3 to 5 m)
Coloration: Dark brown/olive with
  blackish bands and blotches on the
  body
Range: Malay Peninsula, Thailand,
  Sumatra, Borneo, Java, and Sulawesi
Reproduction: 20 to 60 eggs per nest
Diet: Fish, insects, crabs, macaques,
  and other small mammals
International status: Endangered

ing its heart rate. As the heart beats quicker, blood flows faster and oxygen races through the body. On an underwater dive, a crocodile slows its heartbeat and reduces the amount of blood oxygen used.

KEYSTONE SPECIES

Crocodiles are keystone species in their environments. A keystone species is one that is necessary for the survival of many other species within its habitat. Crocodiles feed and release waste in the waters in which they swim. Leftover bits of food feed other smaller species, such as wading birds, crabs, and fish. Crocodile waste puts nutrients into the water and feeds water plants. Reeds and other water plants feed many animals and provide a nursery for others. The young of insects, snails, and fish hatch and feed among the reeds.

Crocodiles are essential for keeping wetland waterways open and for helping their habitat survive during droughts. Crocodiles work like narrow bulldozers, pushing mud out of the way to make deeper channels. They wiggle, squirm, and spin to enlarge their water holes when water becomes scarce. Fish, frogs, and other species need crocodile holes to survive. Without crocodiles, many wetlands environments around the world would not thrive.

Young Nile crocodiles venture out of their burrow.

Chapter Three

Mother of the Year

Beside a **reservoir** in India, a female mugger prepares her first nest. She is six years old and has just become mature enough to produce young. She digs a tunnel-shaped nest in the mud and deposits thirty eggs in the nest, about average for a mugger. Then she uses her powerful legs to cover the nest with soil.

Our mother is a concerned parent. She has a heavy, wide snout and a thick, armored back. She defends her nest successfully against any **predators.** A mugger easily defeats hungry rats, jackals, snakes, and otters.

The hatchlings break through their eggs after fifty-five to seventy-five days. They need their mother's help to emerge from the nest, and she quickly removes the dirt cover. If she does not, her babies may die. The mother opens her mouth, and the 1-foot-long (30-centimeter-long) hatchlings climb in. She gently carries the hatchlings to the water. All crocodile mothers show the same concern for their young. Many hatchlings remain near their mothers for up to two years. Most crocodilian mothers do not

feed their young, but they do protect them from being eaten by predators.

Despite their mothers' care, crocodile eggs and hatchlings have a 90 to 95 percent death rate. Some eggs die in the nest because of heat, drought, or flood. The list of predators

A female mugger crocodile lays her eggs in Tamil Nadu, India.

that attack eggs and hatchlings seems endless. Each crocodile species has different enemies, depending on its location. Common predators include leopards, bears, wild pigs, dogs, foxes, raccoons, opossums, skunks, mongooses, monkeys, baboons, rats, lizards, snakes, birds, turtles, and fish. Even ants can kill the eggs in a crocodile nest.

In Florida, American alligators often lay their eggs in sand traps or beside water traps on golf courses. Florida is also home to billions of fire ants. It is not uncommon to find crocodilian nests swarming with fire ants. The ants devour the eggs and even live hatchlings.

Crocodiles live long lives, although scientists have studied many crocodile species and still do not know exactly how long they live in the wild. It is believed that adults may live sixty to eighty years or more. There have been reports of some crocodiles in zoos living more than one hundred years.

Crocodiles are **opportunistic feeders.** When the opportunity to feed arrives, they eat. They are also **carnivores.** Small crocodiles feed on insects, small fish,

tadpoles, snails, and crabs. As they grow, crocodiles feed on larger animals such as fish, wading birds, snakes, lizards, and small mammals. Adults eat large fish and animals as big as zebras, wildebeests, and even water buffalos.

A crocodile in South Africa captures a meal. Crocodiles eat fish and many other kinds of prey.

Hunting is a time-consuming affair because a crocodile puts in no more effort than necessary to catch its prey. Often, a crocodile will simply float in the water waiting for a thirsty creature to drink. When the prey comes by, the crocodile employs one of three techniques to catch its meal: it lunges from underwater in a surprise attack, it scans the water with its mouth agape, or it grips its victim and spins it in a death roll.

Some crocodiles can leap up to 5 feet (1.5 m) into the air to capture birds or bats. This technique is also good for catching monkeys in trees. Other crocodiles trawl for food by sweeping their open mouths through the water. Any fish foolish enough to swim too close to the crocodile gets clamped in its strong jaws.

Small meals are eaten whole. Only major prey is shared. If the skin is tough or the animal large, crocodiles will share the **carcass.** A zebra, for example, is a shared feast. Crocodiles grab the zebra's flesh with their teeth and tear off pieces of meat.

The home range of a crocodile is shared with many others of its species. Once a crocodile reaches adult size, it is usually perfectly safe among its fellow crocodiles. False gharials, for example, gather in the water or sun

themselves on banks, lying one upon the other like pickup sticks.

Crocodiles are most at home in the water, where they can swim quickly. They move through the water in a neat S-shaped motion. A crocodile's strong tail powers the animal through the water. The limbs act like paddles for steering at slow speeds.

American Crocodile Fast Facts
(Crocodylus acutus)
Adult length: Males: 7 to 15 feet
(2.1 to 4.6 m)
Coloration: 7 to 15 feet (2.1 to 4.6 m)
Range: Florida, Caribbean Islands, Mexico, Belize, Venezuela, Ecuador, Peru, and Colombia
Reproduction: 30 to 60 eggs per nest
Diet: Fish, turtles, crabs, shorebirds, and wading birds
International status: Endangered

A crocodile attacks a wildebeest on the Masai Mara Reserve in Kenya.

Crocodiles can run quickly on land, reaching speeds up to 10 miles (16 km) per hour over short distances. Like snakes, they slither over the mud on their bellies. They can slide down chutes into the water with ease.

Land and water are essential elements for a crocodile's life. It needs both to regulate its temperature. Like all reptiles, crocodiles cannot control their temperature internally. They lie in the sun to warm up and enter the water to cool off. They rest and sleep on land or in the water. Hunting is most often a water activity, yet eating can take place on either water or land. This land-water existence makes crocodiles **amphibious.** Crocodiles have enjoyed this unusual lifestyle for millions of years.

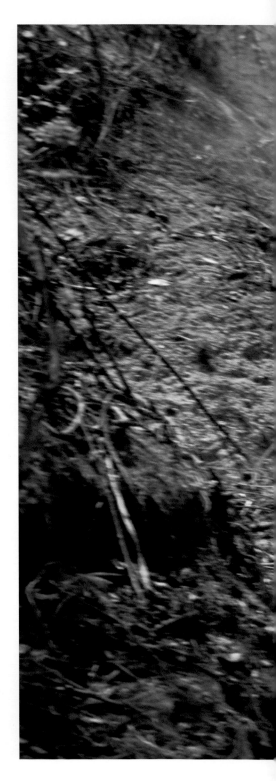

A crocodile runs near the Shire River in Malawi. Though they are most at home in the water, crocodiles can run quickly for short distances on land.

23

Chapter Four

Crocodile Traditions

Crocodiles have existed for more than 200 million years. Early crocodiles were gigantic animals, much larger than today's versions. Crocodiles roamed the waters long before the continents were fully formed. They existed through the time of dinosaurs, into the era of mammals—including humans.

Early people admired the crocodile's power. They feared the beast and they honored it in religious rites. They drew the crocodile's image on cave walls and carved it into stones.

In about 2400 B.C., the Egyptians honored Sobek, a god that was half man and half crocodile. They made sacrifices in Sobek's honor at temples dedicated to his worship. One of the greatest temples stood in Crocodopolis—the city of crocodiles. In those temples, huge Nile crocodiles covered with gold and jewels swarmed in pools. The crocodiles wore bracelets on their front legs and attendants fed the animals daily to keep them happy.

Sobek was half man and half crocodile. The ancient Egyptians believed that he controlled the waters of the Nile River.

Read It!
About 110 million years ago, a gigantic crocodile roamed the earth. In 2000, a fossil of a "super croc" was found in the desert of Niger. *Sarcosuchus imperator* ("flesh crocodile emperor") weighed 10 tons and measured roughly 40 feet (12 m) long. Read all about it in *Super Croc and the Origin of Crocodiles* by Christopher Sloan (National Geographic, 2002).

When a temple crocodile died, it was made into a mummy. It was the ancient Egyptian's burial practice to dry out a human or animal body, remove its inner organs, and embalm the body for burial. The Egyptians mummified adult and **juvenile** crocodiles. They even mummified crocodile eggs. Mummified remains were wrapped in papyrus and linen and placed in tombs.

SOUTHEAST ASIA

Southeast Asians have always lived with crocodiles in their midst. At one time in the Philippines, the Philippine crocodile was believed to be the spirit of an early ruler. The people believed that no crocodile should be killed because the killing might anger that ancient crocodile ruler.

In Sulawesi, the Toraja people believe that crocodiles may be dead family members that have come back to life. They call crocodiles "grandfather." The Toraja think that crocodiles never kill anyone unless that person deserves death. Their god, Poe Mpalaburu, orders the crocodile to take certain people. They believe that sometimes the killing of a human by a crocodile settles an old debt. The Toraja people are most likely to encounter saltwater crocodiles and Siamese crocodiles.

In Borneo, crocodiles were once considered to be guardian angels. But the young girls of West Timor would

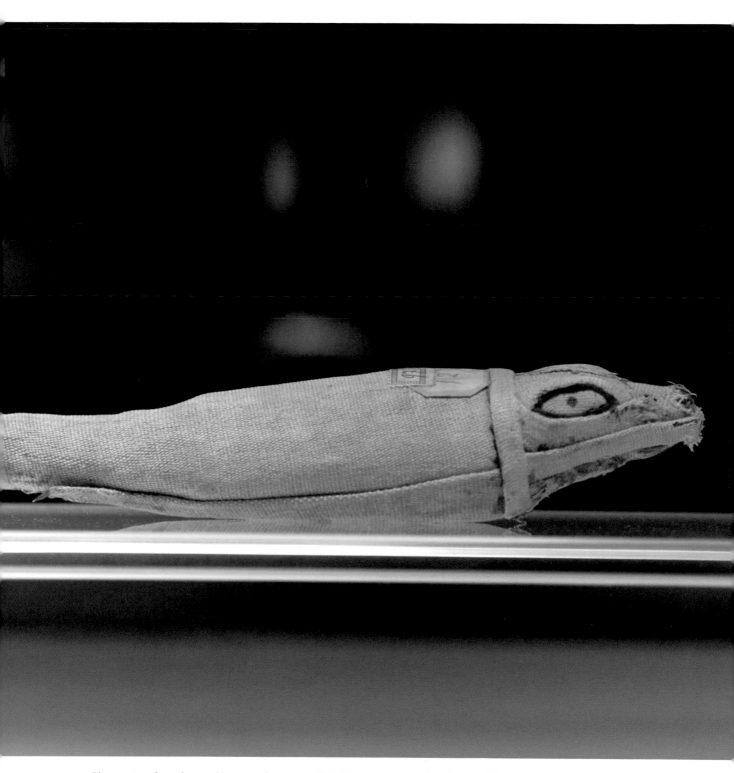

The remains of temple crocodiles were often mummified. This is a mummy of a baby crocodile on display in Luxor, Egypt.

not be likely to think of crocodiles in the same way. Until the late 1800s, Timorese princes believed that they were the descendants of crocodiles. They chose young Timorese girls to be brides for their crocodile ancestors. The girls were dressed up and adorned with jewels, then given to the crocodiles to be eaten.

AFRICA

African traditions and crocodiles go back many centuries. Crocodiles are considered sacred by many tribes. They are believed to be the spirits of the dead that return to protect their old home villages. For this protection, crocodiles are honored.

The Ganda people's interest in crocodiles was a bit grisly until the nineteenth century. For them, the crocodiles living on an island in Lake Victoria offered a way to get rid of their enemies. After a battle, the enemy's dead bodies were tossed onto the island, a human feast for the crocs.

Rock carvings and paintings of crocodiles are

Johnston's Crocodile Fast Facts
(Crocodylus johnstonii)
Adult length: Up to 10 feet (3 m)
Coloration: Brown with black bands on tail and body
Range: Tropical northern Australia
Reproduction: 4 to 20 eggs per nest
Diet: Fish, invertebrates, and small animals of many types
International status: Threatened

found in many regions of Africa. The Nile crocodile ranges from the Nile River to southern Africa. While it dominates the continent, it is not the only crocodile in Africa. Others include the African slender-snouted crocodile and the African dwarf crocodile.

AUSTRALIA

Australia is also home to crocodiles. It hosts the saltwater crocodile and the Johnston's crocodile. The saltwater crocodile is extremely dangerous and sometimes eats humans.

The African slender-snouted crocodile can be found in Central and West Africa.

For this and other reasons, Australia's **aborigines** have a healthy respect for the crocodile.

The Murinbata clan claims the Johnston's crocodile as a protective symbol or totem. They call that species "old man crocodile." The crocodile appears in many Australian folktales. One tale tells the story of the creation of the Liverpool River:

In ancient times, a great crocodile lived in the mountains behind Arnhem Land. One day, the crocodile rose up from the mountains and opened its great mouth. It proceeded to eat the land in large mouthfuls. Bit by bit, the crocodile ate its way to the sea, leaving behind a wide river for fish to live in and man to travel on.

It is not surprising that so many cultures admire and honor the crocodile. Its strength, patience, fierce hunting skills, and endurance have been the basis of many stories and legends. Yet other cultures did not see the power and beauty of the crocodile. Instead, they saw handbags and shoes, belts and wallets, and huge profits.

Australian Aboriginal art includes rock paintings, such as this scene of a crocodile hunt.

Chapter Five

Humans and Crocodiles

For centuries, people hunted crocodiles for food. They ate crocodile meat and used the skins for leather goods. They ground bones and internal organ meat for medicine. They strung crocodile teeth to make necklaces. Nothing was wasted, but careful use of crocodiles changed with time.

In the 1800s, adventurers began hunting crocodiles solely for their skins. Skins were turned into ladies' handbags, gentlemen's belts, book covers, and chair coverings. Young crocodiles were killed and stuffed to put on display in living rooms. The slaughter of young and old reptiles numbered in the millions.

Hunting continued into the 1950s, when it was stylish to wear crocodile shoes and carry a matching handbag. As with many of Mother Nature's creatures, crocodiles lost their lives so that humans could dress up in their skins. By the 1970s, **conservation** groups realized that crocodiles faced **extinction** unless something was done to protect them. Laws were passed to stop hunting.

THREATS TO SURVIVAL

Two major activities continue to threaten crocodile and alligator populations: habitat loss and hunting or poaching. As human populations grow, the need for land on which to live and grow crops increases. One way to get more land is to drain wetlands and use the land for farms or homes. While this suits humans, it destroys natural crocodile habitats. This practice is used throughout the world, and crocodiles suffer as wetlands disappear.

Another human activity that damages crocodile habitats is the damming of streams and rivers. Engineers plan and build reservoirs to hold freshwater. They dam up a river and form a new lake. The newly arranged water system takes away natural habitat and destroys some nesting sites downstream.

Crocodiles have adapted to change for millions of years. Habitat loss is a serious problem that crocodiles solve by finding new homes. They take over drainage ditches, irrigation channels, reservoirs, and ponds on golf courses. Some shocked homeowners have even found alligators in their swimming pools. For a croc, water is water.

Hunting and poaching—which is illegal hunting—have taken their toll on crocodiles. Today, laws protect crocodiles from hunters. It is difficult, however, to convince a poacher that killing a crocodile for its skin is a

Crocodiles rest near a water trap on a golf course. When humans take over crocodile habitat, the crocodiles often learn to live in their new surroundings.

bad thing. One night's hunting and skinning provides a poacher with more money than he could earn in six months of factory work. For poachers in southeast Asia or Africa, illegal hunting may be the only thing that saves their families from hunger.

FIXING THE PROBLEM

Several conservation groups and governments have set up farms to breed crocodiles. They feed and care for the crocs and keep the young separate from the adults to ensure their survival. When the crocodiles reach adulthood, they are slaughtered and their skins and meat are sold to earn money.

In Zimbabwe, the government gives farmers licenses to collect crocodile eggs from nests. Because more than 90 percent of eggs and hatchlings do not survive in the wild, these collected eggs do not reduce the wild population. Instead, they increase it. Farmers must raise all hatchlings to adult size, then return 2 percent of their crocodiles to the wild. The success of the Zimbabwe crocodile farming program is demonstrated by the country's healthy population of Nile crocodiles—nearly fifty thousand strong. And the farmed crocodile population allows farmers to make a tidy profit by selling skins and meat.

Similar programs in Australia, Venezuela, India, and New Guinea are returning the populations of some species to safe numbers. In India, the Madras Crocodile Bank concentrates solely on conservation of crocodiles. They study mostly muggers and saltwater crocodiles.

International laws restrict hunting and killing crocodiles. Legal and conservation efforts do make a difference. Nile, Johnston's, saltwater, New Guinea, and dwarf crocodiles are slowly recovering. Many species show success in parts of their range. With some help, crocodile populations can recover in the wild. Since 1971, the Nile crocodile, Australia's saltwater crocodile, and several other species have been upgraded from endangered to threatened in parts of their ranges. Many scientists believe that continued care may save all crocodilians from extinction.

Saltwater Crocodile Fast Facts
(Crocodylus porosus)
Adult length: 10 to 15 feet (3 m to 5 m)
Coloration: Dark with tan and gray areas; yellow to white belly
Range: Australia, Bangladesh, Brunei, Myanmar (Burma), Cambodia, China, India (including Andaman Islands), Indonesia, Palau (Caroline Islands), Papua New Guinea, Philippines, Solomon Islands, Vanuatu (Banks Islands), and Vietnam
Reproduction: 40 to 70 eggs per nest
Diet: Crabs, turtles, goannas, snakes, shorebirds, and wading birds; large adults occasionally eat water buffalo, cattle, wild boars, and monkeys
International status: Threatened in Australia, Papua New Guinea, and Indonesia; endangered elsewhere

Dwarf crocodiles sometimes dig burrows that have underwater entrances.

Glossary

aborigines (ab-uh-RIJ-uh-neez) one of the first or earliest people to live in a place

amphibious (am-FIB-ee-us) able to live in water and on land

carcass (KAR-kuhss) the body of a dead animal

carnivores (KAR-nuh-vorz) meat eaters

conservation (kon-sur-VAY-shuhn) the act of saving or preserving some aspect of wildlife

extinction (ek-STINGKT-shuhn) the state of a plant or animal no longer existing

juvenile (JOO-vuh-nuhl) a young animal, like a human toddler

nutrients (NOO-tree-uhnts) the minerals, vitamins, and other values in food

opportunistic feeders (op-ur-too-NISS-tik FEE-durz) ones that take advantage of any food available

predators (PRED-uh-turz) animals that hunt and kill other animals for food

reservoir (REH-zuh-vwar) a water source made by humans

successional (suhk-SESH-uhn-uhl) replacing the one before

For More Information

Watch It

Crocodiles: Here Be Dragons. VHS (Alexandria, Va., National Geographic, 1990).

Last Feast of the Crocodiles. VHS (Alexandria, Va., National Geographic, 1996).

Read It

Cheatham, Karyn Follis. *The Crocodile.* San Diego: Lucent Books, 2001.

Jango-Cohen, Judith. *Crocodiles.* New York: Benchmark Books, 2003.

Trueit, Trudi Strain. *Alligators and Crocodiles.* Danbury, Conn.: Children's Press, 2003.

Look It Up

Visit our home page for lots of links about crocodiles: *http://www.childsworld.com/links*

Note to Parents, Teachers, and Librarians: We routinely verify our Web links to make sure they are safe, active sites—so encourage your readers to check them out!

The Animal Kingdom
Where Do Crocodiles Fit In?

Kingdom: Animalia

Phylum: Chordata

Class: Reptilia

Order: Crocodylia

Family: Alligatoridae, Crocodylidae, Gavialidae

Species: 22 or 23 species of crocodilians and 14 species of crocodiles

Index

About the Author

Sophie Lockwood is a former teacher and a longtime writer. She writes textbooks, newspaper articles, and magazine articles. Sophie enjoys writing about animals and their habits. The most interesting part of her research, Sophie says, is learning how scientists apply their knowledge to save endangered species. She lives with her husband in the foothills of the Blue Ridge Mountains.